TABLE OF CONTENTS

01 | SOUP

02 | MEAT

03 | FISH

04 | SALAD

05 | DESSERT RECIPES

SOUP

- Preparation time: 10 min
- Cooking time: 15 min
- Servings: 4

NUTRITION:

- Calories: 172
- Fat: 5 g
- Protein: 6 g
- Carbohydrates: 30 g
- Sugars: 13 g
- Fiber: 8 g
- Sodium: 601 mg

INGREDIENTS

- 1 tablespoon extra-virgin olive oil
- 1 medium onion, chopped
- 2 carrots, finely chopped
- 3 garlic cloves, minced
- 4 cups low-sodium vegetable broth
- 1 (28-ounce / 794-g) can crushed tomatoes
- 1/2 teaspoon dried oregano
- 1/4 teaspoon dried basil
- 4 cups chopped baby kale leaves
- 1/4 teaspoon salt

DIRECTION

1. In a large pot, heat the oil over medium heat. Add the onion and carrots to the pan. Sauté for 3 to 5 minutes until they begin to soften. Add the garlic and sauté for 30 seconds more, until fragrant.
2. Add the vegetable broth, tomatoes, oregano, and basil to the pot and bring to a boil. Reduce the heat to low and simmer for 5 minutes.
3. Using an immersion blender, purée the soup.
4. Add the kale and simmer for 3 more minutes. Season with the salt. Serve immediately.

GUINNESS BEEF STEW WITH CAULIFLOWER MASH

Preparation time: 10 min
Cooking time: 4hr
Servings: 4

NUTRITION:

- Calories: 564
- Fat: 28.0 g
- Protein: 75.2 g
- Carbohydrates: 17.1 g
- Fiber: 5.9 g
- Sugar: 7.1 g

INGREDIENTS

- 2 pounds (907 g) beef round steak, cut into 1-inch cubes
- 1 large head cauliflower, separated into florets
- 5 sprigs fresh thyme
- 1 medium carrot, cut into 1/2-inch pieces
- 1 stick of celery, cut into 1/2-inch pieces
- 1 cup yellow onion, cut into large pieces
- 2/3 cup Guinness
- 1 tablespoon margarine
- 2 cups low sodium beef broth
- 2 tablespoons arrowroot starch
- 1 tablespoon plus 1 teaspoon garlic, diced fine
- 2 teaspoons olive oil
- Sea salt and pepper to taste

DIRECTION

1. Add oil to a large nonstick skillet and heat over medium-high heat. Add beef and sear on all sides. Transfer to crock pot.
2. Add thyme, Guinness, carrot, onion, celery, garlic, and broth. Set to low and cook 6 to 8 hours, or 4 to 5 on high.
3. One hour before the stew is ready, mix arrowroot with 1 ½ tablespoon water and stir into stew.
4. For the mash: bring 2 cups water to a boil in a large pot and add cauliflower. Cover and cook 10 to 12 minutes, or until cauliflower is soft.
5. Drain. Add salt, pepper, 1 teaspoon garlic, and margarine. Use an immersion blender and process until it resembles mashed potatoes.
6. To serve: ladle stew in a bowl and spoon about 1/4 cup of the mash on top. Garnish with fresh thyme, parsley, and cracked pepper if desired.

Broccoli and Chicken Soup

Preparation time: 35 min
Cooking time: 30 min
Servings: 4

INGREDIENTS

- 4 boneless chicken thighs, diced
- 1 small carrot, chopped
- 1 broccoli head, broken into florets
- 1 garlic clove, chopped
- 1 small onion, chopped
- 4 cups water
- 3 tbsp extra virgin olive oil
- 1/2 tsp salt
- black pepper, to taste

Nutrition:

- Calories: 498
- Fat: 34.41 g
- Protein: 25.22 g
- Carbohydrates: 22.01 g
- Fiber: 0.7 g
- Sodium: 1476 mg

DIRECTION

1. In a deep soup pot, heat olive oil and gently sauté broccoli for 2-3 minutes, stirring occasionally. Add in onion, carrot, chicken and cook, stirring for 2-3 minutes. Stir in salt, black pepper and water.
2. Bring to a boil. Simmer for 30 minutes then remove from heat and set aside to cool.
3. In a blender or food processor, blend soup until completely smooth. Serve and enjoy!

CREAMY CHICKEN SOUP

- Preparation time: 35 min
- Cooking time: 30 min
- Servings: 4

NUTRITION:

- Calories: 557
- Fat: 28.44 g
- Protein: 66.22 g
- Carbohydrates: 5.84 g
- Fiber: 1.8 g
- Sodium: 516 mg

INGREDIENTS

- 4 chicken breasts
- 1 carrot, chopped
- 1 cup zucchini, peeled and chopped
- 2 cups cauliflower, broken into florets
- 1 celery rib, chopped
- 1 small onion, chopped
- 5 cups water
- 1/2 tsp salt
- black pepper, to taste

DIRECTION

1. Place chicken breasts, onion, carrot, celery, cauliflower and zucchini in a deep soup pot. Add in salt, black pepper and 5 cups of water. Stir and bring to a boil.
2. Simmer for 30 minutes then remove chicken from the pot and let it cool slightly.
3. Blend soup until completely smooth. Shred or dice the chicken meat, return it back to the pot, stir, and serve.

Quick Clam Chowder

Preparation time: 10 min
Cooking time: 15 min
Servings: 4

INGREDIENTS

- 2 tablespoons extra-virgin olive oil
- 3 slices pepper bacon, chopped
- 1 onion, chopped
- 1 red bell pepper, seeded and chopped
- 1 fennel bulb, chopped
- 3 tablespoons flour
- 5 cups low-sodium or unsalted chicken broth
- 6 ounces (170 g) chopped canned clams, undrained
- 1/2 teaspoon sea salt
- 1/2 cup milk

Nutrition:
- Calories: 335
- Fat: 20 g
- Protein: 20 g
- Carbohydrates: 21 g
- Sugars: 6 g
- Fiber: 3 g
- Sodium: 496 mg

DIRECTION

1. In a large pot over medium-high heat, heat the olive oil until it shimmers. Add the bacon and cook, stirring until browned, about 4 minutes. Remove the bacon from the fat with a slotted spoon, and set it aside on a plate.
2. Add the onion, bell pepper, and fennel to the fat in the pot. Cook, stirring occasionally, until the vegetables are soft, about 5 minutes. Add the flour and cook, stirring constantly, for 1 minute. Add the broth, clams, and salt. Bring to a simmer. Cook, stirring until the soup thickens, about 5 minutes more.
3. Stir in the milk and return the bacon to the pot. Cook, stirring 1 minute more.

LENTIL VEGETABLE SOUP

- Preparation time: 10 min
- Cooking time: 15 min
- Servings: 4

NUTRITION:

- Calories: 330
- Fat: 18 g
- Protein: 33 g
- Carbohydrates: 9 g
- Sugars: 5 g
- Fiber: 2 g
- Sodium: 321 mg

INGREDIENTS

- 2 tablespoons extra-virgin olive oil
- 1 onion, finely chopped
- 1 carrot, chopped
- 1 cup chopped kale (stems removed)
- 3 garlic cloves, minced
- 1 cup canned lentils, drained and rinsed
- 5 cups unsalted vegetable broth
- 2 teaspoons dried rosemary (or 1 tablespoon chopped fresh
- rosemary)
- 1/2 teaspoon sea salt
- 1/4 teaspoon freshly ground black pepper

DIRECTION

1. In a large pot over medium-high heat, heat the olive oil until it shimmers. Add the onion and carrot and cook, stirring until the vegetables begin to soften, about 3 minutes. Add the kale and cook for 3 minutes more. Add the garlic and cook, stirring constantly, for 30 seconds.
2. Stir in the lentils, vegetable broth, rosemary, salt, and pepper. Bring to a simmer. Simmer, stirring occasionally, for 5 minutes more.

Taco Soup

Preparation time: 5 min
Cooking time: 20 min
Servings: 4

INGREDIENTS

- Avocado oil cooking spray
- 1 medium red bell pepper, chopped
- 1/2 cup chopped yellow onion
- 1 pound (454 g) 93% lean ground beef
- 1 teaspoon ground cumin
- 1/2 teaspoon salt
- 1/2 teaspoon chili powder
- 1/2 teaspoon garlic powder
- 2 cups low-sodium beef broth
- 1 (15-ounce / 425-g) can no-salt-added diced tomatoes
- 1 1/2 cup frozen corn
- 1/3 cup half-and-half

Nutrition:
- Calories: 330
- Fat: 18 g
- Protein: 33 g
- Carbohydrates: 9 g
- Sugars: 5 g
- Fiber: 2 g
- Sodium: 321 mg

DIRECTION

1. Heat a large stockpot over medium-low heat. When hot, coat the cooking surface with cooking spray. Put the pepper and onion in the pan and cook for 5 minutes.
2. Add the ground beef, cumin, salt, chili powder, and garlic powder. Cook for 5 to 7 minutes, stirring and breaking apart the beef as needed.
3. Add the broth, diced tomatoes with their juices, and corn. Increase the heat to medium-high and simmer for 10 minutes.
4. Remove from the heat and stir in the half-and-half.

SPLIT PEA SOUP WITH CARROTS

Preparation time: 8 min
Cooking time: 15 min
Servings: 4

NUTRITION:

- Calories: 284
- Fat: 1 g
- Protein: 19 g
- Carbohydrates: 52 g
- Sugars: 9 g
- Fiber: 21 g
- Sodium: 60 mg

INGREDIENTS

- 1 1/2 cups dried green split peas, rinsed and drained
- 4 cups vegetable broth or water
- 2 celery stalks, chopped
- 1 medium onion, chopped
- 2 carrots, chopped
- 3 garlic cloves, minced
- 1 teaspoon herbes de Provence
- 1 teaspoon liquid smoke
- Kosher salt and freshly ground black pepper, to taste
- Shredded carrot, for garnish (optional)

DIRECTION

1. In the electric pressure cooker, combine the peas, broth, celery, onion, carrots, garlic, herbes de Provence, and liquid smoke.
2. Close and lock the lid of the pressure cooker. Set the valve to sealing.
3. Cook on high pressure for 15 minutes.
4. When the cooking is complete, hit Cancel and allow the pressure to release naturally for 10 minutes, then quick release any remaining pressure.
5. Once the pin drops, unlock and remove the lid.
6. Stir the soup and season with salt and pepper.
7. Spoon into serving bowls and sprinkle shredded carrots on top (if using).

Cheeseburger Soup

Preparation time: 15 min
Cooking time: 25 min
Servings: 4

INGREDIENTS

- Avocado oil cooking spray
- 1/2 cup diced white onion
- 1/2 cup diced celery
- 1/2 cup sliced portobello mushrooms
- 1 pound (454 g) 93% lean ground beef
- 1 (15-ounce / 425-g) can no-salt-added diced tomatoes
- 2 cups low-sodium beef broth
- 1/3 cup half-and-half
- 3/4 cup shredded sharp Cheddar cheese

Nutrition:

- Calories: 330
- Fat: 18 g
- Protein: 33 g
- Carbohydrates: 9 g
- Sugars: 5 g
- Fiber: 2 g
- Sodium: 321 mg

DIRECTION

1. Heat a large stockpot over medium-low heat. When hot, coat the cooking surface with cooking spray. Put the onion, celery, and mushrooms into the pot. Cook for 7 minutes, stirring occasionally.
2. Add the ground beef and cook for 5 minutes, stirring and breaking apart as needed.
3. Add the diced tomatoes with their juices and the broth. Increase the heat to medium-high and simmer for 10 minutes.
4. Remove the pot from the heat and stir in the half-and-half.
5. Serve topped with the cheese.

Lime Chicken Tortilla Soup

Preparation time: 10 min
Cooking time: 35 min
Servings: 4

INGREDIENTS

- 1 tablespoon extra-virgin olive oil
- 1 onion, thinly sliced
- 1 garlic clove, minced
- 1 jalapeño pepper, diced
- 2 boneless, skinless chicken breasts
- 4 cups low-sodium chicken broth
- 1 Roma tomato, diced
- 1/2 teaspoon salt
- 2 (6-inch) corn tortillas, cut into thin strips
- Nonstick cooking spray
- Juice of 1 lime
- Minced fresh cilantro, for garnish
- 1/4 cup shredded Cheddar cheese, for garnish

Nutrition:

- Calories: 191
- Fat: 8 g
- Protein: 19 g
- Carbohydrates: 13 g
- Sugars: 2 g
- Fiber: 2 g
- Sodium: 482 mg

DIRECTION

1. In a medium pot, heat the oil over medium-high heat. Add the onion and cook for 3 to 5 minutes until it begins to soften. Add the garlic and jalapeño, and cook until fragrant, about 1 minute more.
2. Add the chicken, chicken broth, tomato, and salt to the pot and bring to a boil. Reduce the heat to medium and simmer gently for 20 to 25 minutes until the chicken breasts are cooked through. Remove the chicken from the pot and set aside.
3. Preheat a broiler to high.
4. Spray the tortilla strips with nonstick cooking spray and toss to coat. Spread in a single layer on a baking sheet and broil for 3 to 5 minutes, flipping once, until crisp.
5. When the chicken is cool enough to handle, shred it with two forks and return to the pot.
6. Season the soup with the lime juice. Serve hot, garnished with cilantro, cheese, and tortilla strips.

THAI SHRIMP SOUP

- Preparation time: 10 min
- Cooking time: 10 min
- Servings: 4

NUTRITION:

- Calories: 189
- Fat: 7 g
- Protein: 8 g
- Carbohydrates: 24 g
- Sugars: 7 g
- Fiber: 7 g
- Sodium: 527 mg

INGREDIENTS

- 1 tablespoon coconut oil
- 1 tablespoon Thai red curry paste
- 1/2 onion, sliced
- 3 garlic cloves, minced
- 2 cups chopped carrots
- 1/2 cup whole unsalted peanuts
- 4 cups low-sodium vegetable broth
- 1/2 cup unsweetened plain almond milk
- 1/2 pound (227 g) shrimp, peeled and deveined
- Minced fresh cilantro, for garnish

DIRECTION

1. In a large pan, heat the oil over medium-high heat until shimmering.
2. Add the curry paste and cook, stirring constantly, for 1 minute. Add the onion, garlic, carrots, and peanuts to the pan, and continue to cook for 2 to 3 minutes until the onion begins to soften.
3. Add the broth and bring to a boil. Reduce the heat to low and simmer for 5 to 6 minutes until the carrots are tender.
4. Using an immersion blender or in a blender, purée the soup until smooth and return it to the pot. With the heat still on low, add the almond milk and stir to combine. Add the shrimp to the pot and cook for 2 to 3 minutes until cooked through.
5. Garnish with cilantro and serve.

MEAT

Roasted Beef with Peppercorn Sauce

Preparation time: 10 min
Cooking time: 90 min
Servings: 4

INGREDIENTS

- 1 1/2 pound top rump beef roast
- 3 teaspoons extra-virgin olive oil
- 3 shallots, minced
- 2 teaspoons minced garlic
- 1 tablespoon green peppercorns
- 2 tablespoons dry sherry
- 2 tablespoons all-purpose flour
- 1 cup sodium-free beef broth

Nutrition:

- Calories 330
- Carbohydrates 4 g
- Protein 36 g

DIRECTION

1. Heat the oven to 300°F.
2. Season the roast with salt and pepper.
3. Position a huge skillet over medium-high heat and add 2 teaspoons of olive oil.
4. Brown the beef on all sides, about 10 minutes in total, and transfer the roast to a baking dish.
5. Roast until desired doneness, about 1 ½ hour for medium. When the roast has been in the oven for 1 hour, start the sauce.
6. In a medium saucepan over medium-high heat, sauté the shallots in the remaining 1 teaspoon of olive oil until translucent, about 4 minutes.
7. Stir in the garlic and peppercorns, and cook for another minute. Whisk in the sherry to deglaze the pan.
8. Whisk in the flour to form a thick paste, cooking for 1 minute and stirring constantly.
9. Fill in the beef broth and whisk for 4 minutes. Season the sauce.
10. Serve the beef with a generous spoonful of sauce.

HERB GARLIC LAMB CHOPS

Preparation time: 5 min
Cooking time: 10 min
Servings: 4

NUTRITION:

- Calories: 168
- Carbohydrates: 12.1 g
- Fat: 2.7 g
- Protein: 23.7 g

INGREDIENTS

- 1/3 cup all-purpose flour
- Ground black pepper, as required
- 1 large egg
- 2 tbsp water
- 2/3 cup cornflakes, crushed
- 1 tbsp parmesan cheese, grated
- 1/8 tsp cayenne pepper
- 1 lb. Cod fillets
- Salt, as required

DIRECTION

1. In a shallow dish, add the flour and black pepper and mix well. In a second shallow dish, add the egg and water and beat well. In a third shallow dish, add the cornflakes, cheese, and cayenne pepper and mix well.
2. Season the cod fillets with salt evenly. Coat the fillets with flour mixture, then dip into the egg mixture and finally coat with the cornflake mixture.
3. Arrange the cod fillets onto the greased cooking rack. Arrange the drip pan in the bottom of the Air Fryer Oven cooking chamber. Select "Air Fry" and then adjust the temperature to 400 °F. Set the time for 10 minutes and press "Start."
4. When the display shows "Add Food" insert the cooking rack in the bottom position. When the display shows "Turn Food" turn the cod fillets. When cooking time is complete, remove the tray from the Air fryer oven. Serve hot.

Coffee-and-Herb-Marinated Steak

Preparation time: 2hr
Cooking time: 10 min
Servings: 3

INGREDIENTS

- 1/4 cup whole coffee beans
- 2 teaspoons garlic
- 2 teaspoons rosemary
- 2 teaspoons thyme
- 1 teaspoon black pepper
- 2 tablespoons apple cider vinegar
- 2 tablespoons extra-virgin olive oil
- 1-pound flank steak, trimmed of visible fat

Nutrition:

- Calories 313
- Fat 20 g
- Protein 31 g

DIRECTION

1. Place the coffee beans, garlic, rosemary, thyme, and black pepper in a coffee grinder or food processor and pulse until coarsely ground.
2. Transfer the coffee mixture to a resealable plastic bag and add the vinegar and oil. Shake to combine.
3. Add the flank steak and squeeze the excess air out of the bag. Seal it. Marinate the steak in the refrigerator for at least 2 hours, occasionally turning the bag over.
4. Preheat the broiler. Line a baking sheet with aluminum foil.
5. Pull the steak out and discard the marinade.
6. Position steak on the baking sheet and broil until it is done to your liking.
7. Put aside for 10 minutes before cutting it.
8. Serve with your favorite side dish.

ROSEMARY LEMON LAMB CHOPS

Preparation time: 10 min
Cooking time: 6 min
Servings: 2

NUTRITION:

- Calories: 260
- Fat: 10.3 g
- Carbohydrates: 1.4 g
- Protein: 38.1 g
- Cholesterol: 122 mg

INGREDIENTS

- 2 lamb chops
- 1 tbsp. dried rosemary
- 2 tbsps. lemon juice

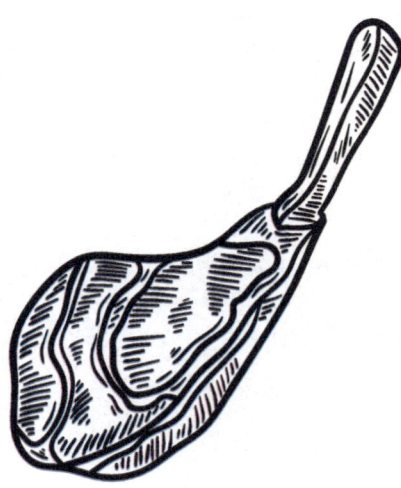

DIRECTION

1. Mix together rosemary and lemon juice and brush over lamb chops.
2. Place the dehydrating tray in a multi-level air fryer basket and place the basket in the instant pot.
3. Place lamb chops on dehydrating tray.
4. Seal pot with air fryer lid and select air fry mode, then set the temperature to 400°F and timer for 6 minutes. Turn lamb chops halfway through.
5. Serve and enjoy.

Pork Chops with Grape Sauce

Preparation time: 15 min
Cooking time: 25 min
Servings: 4

INGREDIENTS

- Cooking spray
- 4 pork chops
- 1/4 cup onion, sliced
- 1 clove garlic, minced
- 1/2 cup low-sodium chicken broth
- 3/4 cup apple juice
- 1 tablespoon cornstarch
- 1 tablespoon balsamic vinegar
- 1 teaspoon honey
- 1 cup seedless red grapes, sliced in half

Nutrition:

- Calories 188;
- Total Fat 4 g
- Saturated Fat 1 g
- Cholesterol 47 mg
- Sodium 117 mg
- Total Carbohydrate 18 g
- Dietary Fiber 1 g
- Total Sugars 13 g
- Protein 19 g
- Potassium 759 mg

DIRECTION

1. Spray oil on your pan.
2. Put it over medium heat.
3. Add the pork chops to the pan.
4. Cook for 5 minutes per side.
5. Remove and set aside.
6. Add onion and garlic.
7. Cook for 2 minutes.
8. Pour in the broth and apple juice.
9. Bring to a boil.
10. Reduce heat to simmer.
11. Put the pork chops back to the skillet.
12. Simmer for 4 minutes.
13. In a bowl, mix the cornstarch, vinegar and honey.
14. Add to the pan.
15. Cook until the sauce has thickened.
16. Add the grapes.
17. Pour sauce over the pork chops before serving.

HERB BUTTER LAMB CHOPS

Preparation time: 10 min
Cooking time: 5 min
Servings: 4

NUTRITION:

- Calories: 278
- Fat: 12.8 g
- Carbohydrates: 0.2 g
- Sugar: 0 g
- Protein: 38 g
- Cholesterol: 129 mg

INGREDIENTS

- 4 lamb chops
- 1 tsp. rosemary, chopped
- 1 tbsp. butter
- Pepper
- Salt

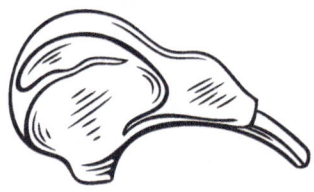

DIRECTION

1. Season lamb chops with pepper and salt.
2. Place the dehydrating tray in a multi-level air fryer basket and place the basket in the instant pot.
3. Place lamb chops on dehydrating tray.
4. Seal pot with air fryer lid and select air fry mode, then set the temperature to 400°F and timer for 5 minutes.
5. Mix together butter and rosemary and spread overcooked lamb chops.
6. Serve and enjoy.

Pork with Cranberry Relish

Preparation time: 30 min
Cooking time: 30 min
Servings: 4

INGREDIENTS

- 12 oz. pork tenderloin, fat trimmed and sliced crosswise
- Salt and pepper to taste
- 1/4 cup all-purpose flour
- 2 tablespoons olive oil
- 1 onion, sliced thinly
- 1/4 cup dried cranberries
- 1/4 cup low-sodium chicken broth
- 1 tablespoon balsamic vinegar

Nutrition:
- Calories 211;
- Total Fat 9 g
- Saturated Fat 2 g
- Cholesterol 53 mg
- Sodium 116 mg
- Total Carbohydrate 15 g
- Dietary Fiber 1 g
- Total Sugars 6 g
- Protein 18 g
- Potassium 378 mg

DIRECTION

1. Flatten each slice of pork using a mallet.
2. In a dish, mix the salt, pepper and flour.
3. Dip each pork slice into the flour mixture.
4. Add oil to a pan over medium-high heat.
5. Cook pork for 3 minutes per side or until golden crispy.
6. Transfer to a serving plate and cover with foil.
7. Cook the onion in the pan for 4 minutes.
8. Stir in the rest of the ingredients.
9. Simmer until the sauce has thickened.

CRISPY CHICKEN WINGS

- Preparation time: 10 min
- Cooking time: 20 min
- Servings: 4

NUTRITION:

- Calories: 275
- Carbohydrates: 9 g
- Fat: 17 g
- Protein: 13 g

INGREDIENTS

- 1 tbsp. gluten-free baking powder
- 3/4 tsp. sea salt
- 2 lbs. chicken wings
- 1/4 tsp. black pepper

DIRECTION

1. Preheat the Air Fryer to 370°F. Merge the chicken wings, baking powder, sea salt, and black pepper.
2. Pour some grease on the Air Fryer basket. Arrange the wings in batches into the Air Fryer basket and cook at 250°F for 15 minutes.
3. Shake the Air Fryer or turn the wings to the other side and cook for another 15 minutes for the wings to be well cooked.
4. Serve.

Creole Braised Sirloin

Preparation time: 15 min
Cooking time: 40 min
Servings: 4

INGREDIENTS

- 1 pound beef round sirloin tip, cut into 4 strips
- 1/4 tsp. freshly ground black pepper
- 2 cups chicken broth (here) or store-bought low-sodium
- chicken broth, divided
- 1 medium onion, chopped
- 1 celery stalk, coarsely chopped
- 1 medium green bell pepper, coarsely chopped
- 2 garlic cloves, minced
- 4 medium tomatoes, coarsely chopped
- 1 bunch mustard greens including stems, coarsely chopped
- 1 tbsp. creole seasoning
- 1/4 tsp. red pepper flakes
- 2 bay leaves

Nutrition:
- Calories: 202
- Total fat: 5 g
- Cholesterol: 60 mg
- Sodium: 129 mg
- Total Carbohydrates: 14 g
- Protein: 28 g

DIRECTION

1. Preheat the oven to 450°F.
2. Massage the beef all over with black pepper.
3. In a Dutch oven, bring 1 cup of broth to a simmer over medium heat.
4. Add the onion, celery, bell pepper, and garlic and cook, stirring often, for 5 minutes, or until the vegetables are softened.
5. Add the tomatoes, mustard greens, Creole seasoning and red pepper flakes and cook for 3 to 5 minutes, or until the greens are wilted.
6. Add the bay leaves, beef, and remaining 1 cup of broth.
7. Cover the pot, transfer to the oven, and cook for 30 minutes or until the juices run clear when you pierce the beef.
8. Remove the beef from the oven and let rest for 5 to 7 minutes. Discard the bay leaves.
9. Thinly slice the beef and serve.

BACON & CHICKEN PATTIES

Preparation time: 5 min
Cooking time: 15 min
Servings: 4

NUTRITION:

- Calories: 387
- Carbohydrates: 13 g
- Fat: 16 g
- Protein: 34 g
- Fiber: 28 g

INGREDIENTS

- 1 1/2 oz. can chicken breast
- 4 slices bacon
- 1/4 cup parmesan cheese
- 1 large egg
- 3 tablespoon flour

DIRECTION

1. Cook the bacon until crispy.
2. Chop the chicken and bacon together in a food processor until fine.
3. Add in the parmesan, egg flour, and blend.
4. Make the patties by hand and fry on medium heat in a pan with some oil.
5. Once browned, flip over, continue cooking and lay them to empty. Serve!

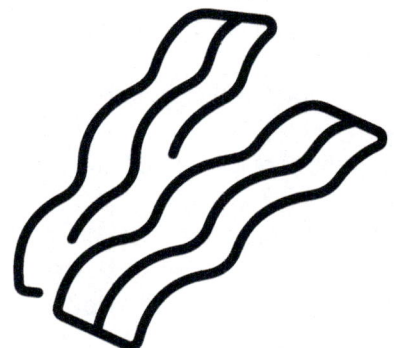

Garlic Chicken Balls

Preparation time: 15 min
Cooking time: 10 min
Servings: 4

INGREDIENTS

- 2 cups ground chicken
- 1 teaspoon minced garlic
- 1 teaspoon dried dill
- 1/3 carrot, grated
- 1 egg beaten
- 1 tablespoon olive oil
- 1/4 cup coconut flakes
- 1/2 teaspoon salt

Nutrition:

- Calories 200
- Fat 11.5
- Fiber 0.6
- Carbs 1.7
- Protein 21.9

DIRECTION

1. In the mixing bowl, mix up together ground chicken, minced garlic, dried dill, carrot, egg and salt.
2. Stir the chicken mixture with the assistance of the fingertips until homogeneous.
3. Then, make medium balls from the mixture.
4. Coat every chicken ball in coconut flakes.
5. Heat vegetable oil in the skillet.
6. Add chicken balls and cook them for 3 minutes from all sides. The cooked chicken balls will have a golden-brown color.

ITALIAN PORK CHOPS

Preparation time: 5 min
Cooking time: 25 min
Servings: 4

NUTRITION:

- Calories 405
- Fat 17 g
- Total carbs 16 g
- Sugar 7.5 g
- Protein 43.5 g
- Sodium 1275 mg

INGREDIENTS

- 4 cloves garlic, sliced
- 4 thick pork chops, fat trimmed
- 1 small yellow onion, cut into rings
- 1/2 cup low-fat mozzarella cheese
- 1 (28-ounce) can diced tomatoes
- 1 teaspoon paprika
- 1 teaspoon dried oregano
- 1 chicken bouillon cube
- Salt and pepper to taste

DIRECTION

1. Preheat the oven to 400°F (200°C). Grease a baking pan with some cooking spray.
2. Season the pork chops with pepper.
3. Grease a medium saucepan or skillet with cooking spray and heat it over medium heat.
4. Add the pork chops and stir-cook for 2 minutes per side until evenly brown.
5. Add the garlic and onion rings and stir-cook for 1-2 minutes until softened.
6. Add the spices, tomato and bouillon cube; simmer for 2-3 minutes.
7. Pour in the tomato sauce.
8. Add the mixture to the baking pan, top with the cheese, and bake for about 20 minutes until the top is golden brown.
9. Let cool slightly and serve warm.

Tomato Steak Kebabs

Preparation time: 5 min
Cooking time: 15 min
Servings: 4

INGREDIENTS

- 1 teaspoon Dijon mustard
- 1 pound top sirloin steak, cut into 1-inch cubes
- 1/4 cup balsamic vinaigrette
- 2 cups cherry tomatoes
- 1/4 cup barbecue sauce

Nutrition:

- Calories: 498
- Fat: 34.41 g
- Protein: 25.22 g
- Carbohydrates: 22.01 g
- Fiber: 0.7 g
- Sodium: 1476 mg

DIRECTION

1. Add the barbecue sauce, vinaigrette and mustard to a mixing bowl; mix well. Set aside 1/4 of the mixture.
2. Add the beef and coat well.
3. Take four metal or soaked wooden skewers and thread them alternately with tomatoes and beef pieces.
4. Preheat the grill to medium-high heat. Grease the grill rack with cooking spray.
5. Grill the skewers for 6-8 minutes until the beef is tender. When 3-4 minutes remain, begin basting frequently with the reserved mixture.

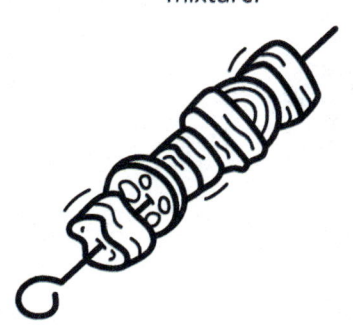

BEEF CHILI

- Preparation time: 10 min
- Cooking time: 20 min
- Servings: 4

NUTRITION:

- Calories: 498
- Fat: 34.41 g
- Protein: 25.22 g
- Carbohydrates: 22.01 g
- Fiber: 0.7 g
- Sodium: 1476 mg

INGREDIENTS

- 1/2 tsp. Garlic Powder
- 1 tsp. Coriander, grounded
- 1 lb. Beef, grounded
- 1/2 tsp. Sea Salt
- 1/2 tsp. Cayenne Pepper
- 1 tsp. Cumin, grounded
- 1/2 tsp. Pepper, grounded
- 1/2 cup Salsa, low-carb & no-sugar

DIRECTION

1. Heat a large-sized pan over medium-high heat and cook the beef in it until browned.
2. Stir in all the spices and cook them for 7 minutes or until everything is combined.
3. When the beef gets cooked, spoon in the salsa.
4. Bring the mixture to a simmer and cook for another 8 minutes or until everything comes together.
5. Take it from heat and transfer to a serving bowl.

3
FISH

BUTTER COD WITH LEMONY ASPARAGUS

- Preparation time: 5 min
- Cooking time: 10 min
- Servings: 4

NUTRITION:

- Calories 200
- Fat 11.5
- Fiber 0.6
- Carbs 1.7
- Protein 21.9

INGREDIENTS

- 4 (4-ounce / 113-g) cod fillets
- 1/4 teaspoon garlic powder
- 1/4 teaspoon salt
- 1/4 teaspoons freshly ground black pepper
- 2 tablespoons unsalted butter
- 24 asparagus spears, woody ends trimmed
- 1/2 cup brown rice, cooked
- 1 tablespoon freshly squeezed lemon juice

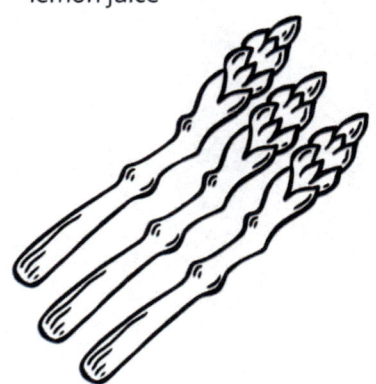

DIRECTION

1. In a large bowl, season the cod fillets with the garlic powder, salt, and pepper. Set aside.
2. Melt the butter in a skillet over medium-low heat.
3. Place the cod fillets and asparagus in the skillet in a single layer. Cook covered for 8 minutes, or until the cod is cooked through.
4. Divide the cooked brown rice, cod fillets, and asparagus among four plates. Serve drizzled with the lemon juice.

Halibut Ceviche with Cilantro

Preparation time: 10 min
Cooking time: 0 min
Servings: 4

INGREDIENTS

- 1/2 pound (227 g) fresh skinless, white, ocean fish fillet (halibut, mahi mahi, etc.), diced
- 1 cup freshly squeezed lime juice, divided
- 2 tablespoons chopped fresh cilantro, divided
- 1 Serrano pepper, sliced
- 1 garlic clove, crushed
- 3/4 teaspoon salt, divided
- 1/2 red onion, thinly sliced
- 2 tomatoes, diced
- 1 red bell pepper, seeded and diced
- 1 tablespoon extra-virgin olive oil

Nutrition:
- Calories: 122
- Fat: 4.1 g
- Protein: 11.9 g
- Carbs: 11.1 g
- Fiber: 2.1 g
- Sugar: 4.9 g
- Sodium: 404 mg

DIRECTION

1. In a large mixing bowl, combine the fish, 3/4 cup of lime juice, 1 tablespoon of cilantro, Serrano pepper, garlic, and 1/2 teaspoon of salt.
2. The fish should be covered or nearly covered in lime juice. Cover the bowl and refrigerate for 4 hours.
3. Sprinkle the remaining 1/4 teaspoon of salt over the onion in a small bowl, and let sit for 10 minutes. Drain and rinse well.
4. In a large bowl, combine the tomatoes, bell pepper, olive oil, remaining 1/4 cup of lime juice, and onion. Let rest for at least 10 minutes, or as long as 4 hours, while the fish "cooks."
5. When the fish is ready, it will be completely white and opaque. At this time, strain the juice, reserving it in another bowl. If desired, remove the Serrano pepper and garlic.
6. Add the vegetables to the fish, and stir gently. Taste, and add some of the reserved lime juice to the ceviche as desired.
7. Serve topped with the remaining 1 tablespoon of cilantro.

LEMON CHILI SALMON

- Preparation time: 5 min
- Cooking time: 15 min
- Servings: 4

NUTRITION:

- Calories: 498
- Fat: 34.41 g
- Protein: 25.22 g
- Carbohydrates: 22.01 g
- Fiber: 0.7 g
- Sodium: 1476 mg

INGREDIENTS

- 1 teaspoon Dijon mustard
- 1 pound top sirloin steak, cut into 1-inch cubes
- 1/4 cup balsamic vinaigrette
- 2 cups cherry tomatoes
- 1/4 cup barbecue sauce

DIRECTION

1. Preheat the air fryer to 325° F.
2. Place salmon fillets in an air fryer baking pan and drizzle with olive oil, lemon juice, and orange juice.
3. Sprinkle chili slices over salmon and season with pepper and salt.
4. Place pan in the air fryer and cook for 15-17 minutes.
5. Garnish with dill and serve.

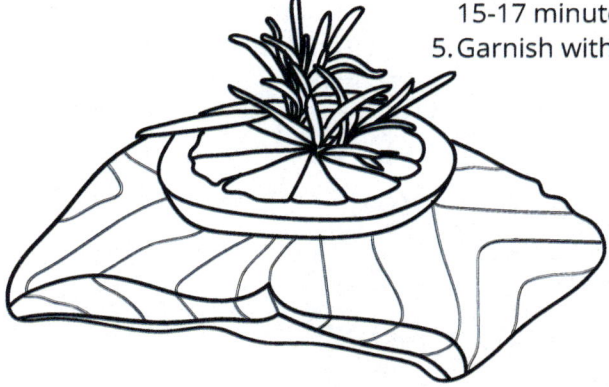

Basil-Parmesan Crusted Salmon

Preparation time: 5 min
Cooking time: 10 min
Servings: 2

INGREDIENTS

- Grated Parmesan: 3 tablespoons
- Skinless four salmon fillets
- Salt: 1/4 teaspoon
- Freshly ground black pepper
- Low-fat mayonnaise: 3 tablespoons
- Basil leaves, chopped
- Half lemon

Nutrition:

- Calories: 289
- Carbohydrates: 1.5 g
- Protein: 30 g
- Fat: 18.5 g

DIRECTION

1. Let the air fryer preheat to 400° F. Spray the basket with olive oil.
2. With salt, pepper, and lemon juice, season the salmon.
3. In a bowl, mix two tablespoons of Parmesan cheese with mayonnaise and basil leaves.
4. Add this mix and more parmesan on top of salmon and cook for seven minutes or until fully cooked.
5. Serve hot.

TUNA BURGERS

- Preparation time: 5 min
- Cooking time: 6 min
- Servings: 4

NUTRITION:

- Calories: 151
- Carbohydrates: 6.3 g
- Fat: 6.4 g
- Protein: 16.4 g

INGREDIENTS

- 7 Oz canned tuna
- 1 large egg
- 1/4 cup breadcrumbs
- 1 tbsp. Mustard
- 1/4 tsp garlic powder
- 1/4 tsp onion powder
- 1/4 tsp cayenne pepper
- Salt and ground black pepper, as required

DIRECTION

1. Add all the ingredients into a bowl and mix until well combined. Make 4 equal-sized patties from the mixture.
2. Arrange the patties onto a greased cooking rack. Arrange the drip pan in the bottom of the Air Fryer Oven cooking chamber. Select "Air Fry" and then adjust the temperature to 400 °F. Set the time for 6 minutes and press "Start."
3. When the display shows "Add Food" insert the cooking rack in the center position.
4. When the display shows "Turn Food" turn the burgers.
5. When the cooking time is complete, remove the tray from the Air fryer oven. Serve hot.

Crispy Fish Sticks in Air Fryer

Preparation time: 10 min
Cooking time: 15 min
Servings: 2

INGREDIENTS

- Whitefish such as cod 1 lb.
- Mayonnaise 1/4 c
- Dijon mustard 2 tbsp.
- Water 2 tbsp.
- Pork rind 1&1/2 c
- Cajun seasoning 3/4 tsp
- Kosher salt& pepper to taste

Nutrition:

- Calories: 263
- Fat: 16 g
- Net Carbohydrates: 1 g
- Protein: 26.4 g

DIRECTION

1. Spray non-stick cooking spray to the air fryer rack.
2. Pat the fish dry & cut into sticks about 1 inch by 2 inches' broad
3. Stir together the mayo, mustard, and water in a tiny small dish. Mix the pork rinds & Cajun seasoning into another small container.
4. Adding kosher salt& pepper to taste (both pork rinds & seasoning can have a decent amount of kosher salt, so you can dip a finger to see how salty it is).
5. Working for one slice of fish at a time, dip to cover in the mayo mix & then tap off the excess. Dip into the mixture of pork rind, then flip to cover. Place on the rack of an air fryer.
6. Set at 400° F to Air Fry & bake for 5 minutes, then turn the fish with tongs and bake for another 5 minutes. Serve.

BREADED COD

⏱ Preparation time: 5 min
🍲 Cooking time: 10 min
🍽 Servings: 4

NUTRITION:

- Calories: 339
- Fat: 17.5 g
- Carbohydrates: 2 g
- Sugar 2 g
- Protein: 44 g

INGREDIENTS

- 1/3 cup all-purpose flour
- Ground black pepper, as required
- 1 large egg
- 2 tbsp water
- 2/3 cup cornflakes, crushed
- 1 tbsp parmesan cheese, grated
- 1/8 tsp cayenne pepper
- 1 lb. Cod fillets
- Salt, as required

DIRECTION

1. In a shallow dish, add the flour and black pepper and mix well. In a second shallow dish, add the egg and water and beat well. In a third shallow dish, add the cornflakes, cheese, and cayenne pepper and mix well.
2. Season the cod fillets with salt evenly. Coat the fillets with flour mixture, then dip into the egg mixture and finally coat with the cornflake mixture.
3. Arrange the cod fillets onto the greased cooking rack. Arrange the drip pan in the bottom of the Air Fryer Oven cooking chamber. Select "Air Fry" and then adjust the temperature to 400 °F. Set the time for 10 minutes and press "Start."
4. When the display shows "Add Food" insert the cooking rack in the bottom position. When the display shows "Turn Food" turn the cod fillets. When cooking time is complete, remove the tray from the Air fryer oven. Serve hot.

Buttered Salmon

Preparation time: 5 min
Cooking time: 10 min
Servings: 2

INGREDIENTS

- 2 salmon fillets (6-oz)
- Salt and ground black pepper, as required
- 1 tbsp butter, melted

Nutrition:

- Calories: 223
- Carbohydrates: 1 g
- Fat: 10.4 g
- Protein: 30 g

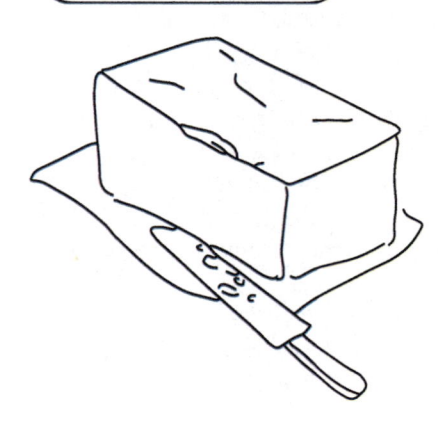

DIRECTION

1. Season each salmon fillet with salt and black pepper and then, coat with the butter. Arrange the salmon fillets onto the greased cooking tray.
2. Arrange the drip pan in the bottom of the Air Fryer Oven cooking chamber. Select "Air Fry" and then adjust the temperature to 360 °F. Set the time for 10 minutes and press "Start."
3. When the display shows "Add Food" insert the cooking tray in the center position. When the display shows "Turn Food" turn the salmon fillets.
4. When cooking time is complete, remove the tray from the Air fryer oven. Serve hot.

SALMON PATTIES

Preparation time: 10 min
Cooking time: 7 min
Servings: 2

NUTRITION:

- Calories: 184
- Fat: 9.2 g
- Carbohydrates: 1 g
- Sugar 0.4 g
- Protein: 24.9 g

INGREDIENTS

- 8 oz. salmon fillet, minced
- 1 lemon, sliced
- 1/2 teaspoon garlic powder
- 1 egg lightly beaten
- 1/8 teaspoon salt

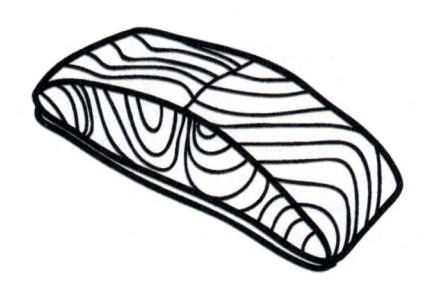

DIRECTION

1. Add all ingredients except lemon slices into the bowl and mix until well combined.
2. Spray air fryer basket with cooking spray.
3. Place lemon slice into the air fryer basket.
4. Make the equal shape of patties from the salmon mixture and place on top of lemon slices into the air fryer basket.
5. Cook at 390 F for 7 minutes.
6. Serve and enjoy.

Spiced Tilapia

Preparation time: 5 min
Cooking time: 12 min
Servings: 4

INGREDIENTS

- 1/2 Tsp lemon pepper seasoning
- 1/2 tsp. Garlic powder
- 1/2 tsp onion powder
- Salt and ground black pepper, as required
- 2 (6-oz) tilapia fillets
- 1 tbsp olive oil

Nutrition:

- Calories: 206
- Carbohydrates: 0.2 g
- Fat: 8.6 g
- Protein: 31.9 g

DIRECTION

1. In a small bowl, mix the spices, salt, and black pepper. Coat the tilapia fillets with oil and then rub with spice mixture. Arrange the tilapia fillets onto a lightly greased cooking rack, skin-side down.
2. Arrange the drip pan in the bottom of the Air Fryer Oven cooking chamber. Select "Air Fry" and then adjust the temperature to 360 °F. Set the time for 12 minutes and press "Start."
3. When the display shows "Add Food" insert the cooking rack in the bottom position. When the display shows "Turn Food" turn the fillets.
4. When cooking time is complete, remove the tray from the Air fryer oven. Serve hot.

SPICY CATFISH

Preparation time: 5 min
Cooking time: 15 min
Servings: 4

NUTRITION:

- Calories: 339
- Fat: 17.5 g
- Carbohydrates: 2 g
- Sugar 2 g
- Protein: 44 g

INGREDIENTS

- 2 tbsp cornmeal polenta
- 2 tsp cajun seasoning
- 1/2 tsp paprika
- 1/2 tsp garlic powder
- Salt, as required
- 2 (6-oz) catfish fillets
- 1 tbsp olive oil

DIRECTION

1. In a bowl, mix the cornmeal, Cajun seasoning paprika, garlic powder, and salt. Add the catfish fillets and coat evenly with the mixture. Now, coat each fillet with oil.
2. Arrange the fish fillets onto a greased cooking rack and spray with cooking spray. Arrange the drip pan in the bottom of the Air Fryer Oven cooking chamber. Select "Air Fry" and then adjust the temperature to 400 °F. Set the timer for 14 minutes and press "Start."
3. When the display shows "Add Food" insert the cooking rack in the center position. When the display shows "Turn Food" turn the fillets.
4. When cooking time is complete, remove the rack from the Air fryer oven. Serve hot.

Spiced Tilapia

Preparation time: 5 min
Cooking time: 12 min
Servings: 4

INGREDIENTS

- 1/2 Tsp lemon pepper seasoning
- 1/2 tsp. Garlic powder
- 1/2 tsp onion powder
- Salt and ground black pepper, as required
- 2 (6-oz) tilapia fillets
- 1 tbsp olive oil

Nutrition:

- Calories: 206
- Carbohydrates: 0.2 g
- Fat: 8.6 g
- Protein: 31.9 g

DIRECTION

1. In a small bowl, mix the spices, salt, and black pepper. Coat the tilapia fillets with oil and then rub with spice mixture. Arrange the tilapia fillets onto a lightly greased cooking rack, skin-side down.
2. Arrange the drip pan in the bottom of the Air Fryer Oven cooking chamber. Select "Air Fry" and then adjust the temperature to 360 °F. Set the time for 12 minutes and press "Start."
3. When the display shows "Add Food" insert the cooking rack in the bottom position. When the display shows "Turn Food" turn the fillets.
4. When cooking time is complete, remove the tray from the Air fryer oven. Serve hot.

Vinegar Halibut

Preparation time: 5 min
Cooking time: 12 min
Servings: 2

INGREDIENTS

- 2 (5-oz) halibut fillets
- 1 garlic clove, minced
- 1 tsp fresh rosemary, minced
- 1 tbsp olive oil
- 1 tbsp red wine vinegar
- 1/8 tsp hot sauce

Nutrition:

- Calories: 223
- Carbohydrates: 1 g
- Fat: 10.4 g
- Protein: 30 g

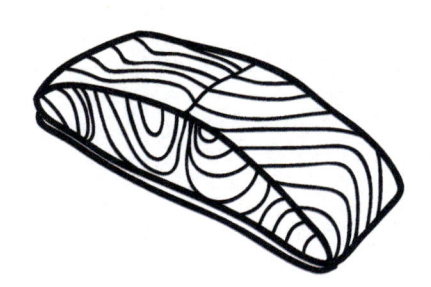

DIRECTION

1. In a large resealable bag add all ingredients. Seal the bag and shale well to mix. Refrigerate to marinate for at least 30 minutes. Remove the fish fillets from the bag and shake off the excess marinade. Arrange the halibut fillets onto the greased cooking tray.
2. Arrange the drip pan in the bottom of the Air Fryer Oven cooking chamber. Select "Bake" and then adjust the temperature to 450 °F. Set the time for 12 minutes and press "Start." When the display shows "Add Food" insert the cooking tray in the center position. When the display shows "Turn Food" turn the halibut fillets. When the cooking time is complete, remove the tray from the Air fryer oven. Serve hot.

BROILED COD FILLETS WITH GARLIC MANGO SALSA

- Preparation time: 10 min
- Cooking time: 10 min
- Servings: 4

NUTRITION:

- Calories: 198
- Fat: 8.1 g
- Protein: 21.2 g
- Carbs: 13.2 g
- Fiber: 2.2 g
- Saturated fat: 1 g
- Sodium: 355 mg

INGREDIENTS

Cod:

- 1 pound (454 g) cod, cut into 4 fillets, pin bones removed
- 2 tablespoons extra-virgin olive oil
- 3/4 teaspoon sea salt, divided

Mango Salsa:

- 1 mango, pitted, peeled, and cut into cubes
- 1/4 cup chopped cilantro
- 1 jalapeño, deseeded and finely chopped
- 1/2 red onion, finely chopped
- Juice of 1 lime
- 1 garlic clove, minced

DIRECTION

1. Preheat the broiler to high. Place the cod fillets on a rimmed baking sheet. Brush both sides of the fillets with the olive oil. Sprinkle with 1/2 teaspoon of the salt.
2. Broil in the preheated broiler for 5 to 10 minutes until the flesh flakes easily with a fork.
3. Meanwhile, make the mango salsa by stirring together the mango, cilantro, jalapeño, red onion, lime juice, garlic, and remaining salt in a small bowl.
4. Serve the cod warm topped with the mango salsa.

FRUITY COD WITH SALSA

⏱ Preparation time: 10 min
🍲 Cooking time: 10 min
🍽 Servings: 4

NUTRITION:

- Calories: 200
- Fat: 8.0 g
- Protein: 21.1 g
- Carbs: 12.9 g
- Fiber: 1.9 g
- Sugar: 7.6 g
- Sodium: 355 mg

INGREDIENTS

- 1 pound (454 g) cod, cut into 4 fillets, pin bones removed
- 2 tablespoons extra-virgin olive oil
- 3/4 teaspoon sea salt, divided
- 1 mango, pitted, peeled, and cut into cubes
- 1/4 cup chopped cilantro
- 1/2 red onion, finely chopped
- 1 jalapeño, seeded and finely chopped
- 1 garlic clove, minced
- Juice of 1 lime

DIRECTION

1. Preheat the oven broiler on high.
2. On a rimmed baking sheet, brush the cod with the olive oil and season with 1/2 teaspoon of the salt. Broil until the fish is opaque, 5 to 10 minutes.
3. Meanwhile, in a small bowl, combine the mango, cilantro, onion, jalapeño, garlic, lime juice, and remaining 1/4 teaspoon of salt.
4. Serve the cod with the salsa spooned over the top.

4
SALAD

TOMATO, CUCUMBER, AND AVOCADO SALAD

Preparation time: 10 min
Cooking time: 0 min
Servings: 4

NUTRITION:

- Calories: 152
- Fat: 12.1 g
- Protein: 2.1 g
- Carbohydrates: 10.9 g
- Fiber: 4.1 g
- Sugar: 4.0 g

INGREDIENTS

- 1 cup cherry tomatoes, halved
- 1 large cucumber, chopped
- 1 small red onion, thinly sliced
- 1 avocado, diced
- 2 tablespoons chopped fresh dill
- 2 tablespoons extra-virgin olive oil
- Juice of 1 lemon
- 1/4 teaspoon salt
- 1/4 teaspoon freshly ground black pepper

DIRECTION

1. In a large mixing bowl, combine the tomatoes, cucumber, onion, avocado, and dill.
2. In a small bowl, combine the oil, lemon juice, salt, and pepper, and mix well.
3. Drizzle the dressing over the vegetables and toss to combine.

Green Salad with Blackberries Vinaigrette

Preparation time: 15 min
Cooking time: 20 min
Servings: 4

INGREDIENTS

For the Vinaigrette:
- 1 pint blackberries
- 2 tablespoons red wine vinegar
- 1 tablespoon honey
- 3 tablespoons extra-virgin olive oil
- 1/4 teaspoon salt
- Freshly ground black pepper

For the Salad:
- 1 sweet potato, cubed
- 1 teaspoon extra-virgin olive oil
- 8 cups salad greens (baby spinach, spicy greens, romaine)
- 1/2 red onion, sliced
- 1/4 cup crumbled goat cheese

Nutrition:
- Calories: 197
- Fat: 12.1 g
- Protein: 3.1 g
- Carbohydrates: 20.9 g
- Fiber: 6.1 g
- Sugar: 10.0 g

DIRECTION

1. To Make the Vinaigrette:
2. In a blender jar, combine the blackberries, vinegar, honey, oil, salt, and pepper, and process until smooth. Set aside.
3. To Make the Salad:
4. Preheat the oven to 425oF (220°C). Line a baking sheet with parchment paper.
5. In a medium mixing bowl, toss the sweet potato with the olive oil. Transfer to the prepared baking sheet and roast for 20 minutes, stirring once halfway through, until tender. Remove and cool for a few minutes.
6. In a large bowl, toss the greens with the red onion and cooled sweet potato, and drizzle with the vinaigrette. Serve topped with 1 tablespoon of goat cheese per serving.

WILD RICE SALAD WITH CRANBERRIES AND ALMONDS

Preparation time: 6 min
Cooking time: 25 min
Servings: 4

NUTRITION:

- Calories: 126
- Carbohydrates: 18 g
- Fiber: 2 g

INGREDIENTS

- For the rice:
- 2 cups wild rice blend, rinsed
- 1 teaspoon kosher salt
- 2 1/2 cups Vegetable Broth
- For the dressing:
- 1/4 cup extra-virgin olive oil
- 1/4 cup white wine vinegar
- 1 1/2 teaspoon grated orange zest
- Juice of 1 medium orange (about 1/4 cup)
- 1 teaspoon honey or pure maple syrup
- For the salad:
- 3/4 cup unsweetened dried cranberries
- 1/2 cup sliced almonds, toasted
- Freshly ground black pepper

Direction

To make the rice
1. In the electric pressure cooker, combine the rice, salt, and broth.
2. Close and lock the lid. Set the valve to sealing.
3. Cook on high pressure for 25 minutes.
4. When the cooking is complete, hit Cancel and allow the pressure to release naturally for 1 minutes, then quick release any remaining pressure.
5. Once the pin drops, unlock and remove the lid.
6. Let the rice cool briefly, then fluff it with a fork.
7. To make the dressing
8. While the rice cooks, make the dressing: In a small jar with a screw-top lid, combine the olive oil, vinegar, zest, juice, and honey. (If you don't have a jar, whisk the ingredients together in a small bowl.) Shake to combine.

To make the salad
1. Mix rice, cranberries, and almonds.
2. Add the dressing and season with pepper.
3. Serve warm or refrigerate.

Summer Salad with Honey Dressing

Preparation time: 5 min
Cooking time: 0 min
Servings: 4

INGREDIENTS

- For the Salad:
- 8 cups mixed greens or preferred lettuce, loosely packed
- 4 cups arugula, loosely packed
- 2 peaches, sliced 1/2 cup thinly sliced red onion
- 1/2 cup chopped walnuts or pecans
- 1/2 cup crumbled feta
- For the Dressing:
- 4 teaspoons extra-virgin olive oil
- 4 teaspoons honey

Nutrition:

- Calories: 264
- Fat: 18.1 g
- Protein: 8.1 g
- Carbohydrates: 21.9 g
- Fiber: 5.1 g
- Sugar: 16.0 g

DIRECTION

1. To Make the Salad:
2. Combine the mixed greens, arugula, peaches, red onion, walnuts, and feta in a large bowl. Divide the salad into four portions.
3. Drizzle the dressing over each individual serving of salad.
4. To Make the Dressing:
5. In a small bowl, whisk together the olive oil and honey.

BUFFALO CHICKEN SALADS

Preparation time: 7 min
Cooking time: 3 hr
Servings: 5

NUTRITION:

- Calories: 92
- Fat: 4.1 g
- Protein: 7.1 g
- Carbohydrates: 6.9 g
- Fiber: 1.1 g
- Sugar: 5.3 g
- Sodium: 388 mg

INGREDIENTS

- 1 1/2 pound chicken breast halves
- 1/2 cup Wing Time Buffalo chicken sauce
- 4 teaspoons cider vinegar
- 1 teaspoon Worcestershire sauce
- 1 teaspoon paprika
- 1/3 cup light mayonnaise
- 2 tablespoons fat-free milk
- 2 tablespoons crumbled blue cheese
- 2 romaine hearts, chopped
- 1 cup whole grain croutons
- 1/2 cup very thinly sliced red onion

DIRECTION

1. Place chicken in a 2-quarts slow cooker. Mix together Worcestershire sauce, 2 teaspoons of vinegar and Buffalo sauce in a small bowl; pour over chicken. Dust with paprika. Close and cook for 3 hours on low-heat setting.
2. Mix the leftover 2 teaspoons of vinegar with milk and light mayonnaise together in a small bowl at serving time; mix in blue cheese. While chicken is still in the slow cooker, pull meat into bite-sized pieces using two forks.
3. Split the romaine among 6 dishes. Spoon sauce and chicken over lettuce. Pour with blue cheese dressing then add red onion slices and croutons on top.

Sofrito Steak and Veg Salad

Preparation time: 15 min
Cooking time: 20 min
Servings: 4

INGREDIENTS

- 4 ounces (113 g) recaíto cooking base
- 2 (4-ounce / 113-g) flank steaks
- 8 cups fresh spinach, loosely packed
- 1/2 cup sliced red onion
- 2 cups diced tomato
- 2 avocados, diced
- 2 cups diced cucumber
- 1/3 cup crumbled feta

Nutrition:
- Calories: 346
- Fat: 18.1 g
- Protein: 25.1 g
- Carbohydrates: 17.9 g
- Fiber: 8.1 g
- Sugar: 6.0 g
- Sodium: 380 mg

DIRECTION

1. Heat a large skillet over medium-low heat. When hot, pour in the recaíto cooking base, add the steaks, and cover. Cook for 8 to 12 minutes.
2. Meanwhile, divide the spinach into four portions. Top each portion with one-quarter of the onion, tomato, avocados, and cucumber.
3. Remove the steak from the skillet, and let it rest for about 2 minutes before slicing. Place one-quarter of the steak and feta on top of each portion.

GRAIN, SEAFOOD, AND FRUIT SALAD

Preparation time: 30 min
Cooking time: 20 min
Servings: 4

NUTRITION:

- Calories: 470
- Fat: 16.0 g
- Protein: 30.0 g
- Carbohydrates: 56.0 g
- Fiber: 10.0 g
- Sugar: 16.0 g
- Sodium: 320 mg

INGREDIENTS

- 1 cup quinoa, rinsed
- 1/2 pound (227 g) medium shrimps, peeled and deveined
- 1/2 pound (227 g) scallops
- 1 tablespoon olive oil
- 1/2 red bell pepper, chopped
- 1 roma plum tomatoes, deseeded and chopped
- 1 jalapeño pepper, stemmed and finely chopped
- 1/2 cup cooked black beans
- 1 mango, chopped
- 1 avocado, chopped
- 2 small scallions, chopped
- 2 tablespoons cilantro leaves, chopped
- Citrus Dressing:
- 2 tablespoons lime juice
- 2 tablespoons orange juice
- 1 teaspoon honey
- 1/4 teaspoon cayenne pepper
- 1 tablespoon extra-virgin olive oil
- Sea salt, to taste

Direction

1. Pour the quinoa in a pot, then pour in enough water to cover. Bring to a boil, then reduce the heat to low and simmer for 10 to 15 minutes or until the liquid has been absorbed. Fluff with a fork and let stand until ready to use.
2. Meanwhile, combine the ingredients for the citrus dressing in a small bowl. Stir to mix well. Set aside until ready to use.
3. Put the shrimps and scallops in a separate bowl, then drizzle with the olive oil. Toss to coat well.
4. Add the oiled shrimps and scallops in a nonstick skillet and grill over medium-high heat for 4 minutes or until opaque. Flip them halfway through. Remove them from the skillet and allow to cool.
5. Combine the cooked quinoa, shrimp and scallops with bell pepper, tomato, jalapeño, beans, mango, avocado, and scallions in a large salad bowl, then drizzle with the citrus dressing. Toss to combine well.
6. Garnish with cilantro leaves and serve immediately.

Cobb Salad

Preparation time: 10 min
Cooking time: 30 min
Servings: 4

INGREDIENTS

For the Salad:
- 8 (2-ounce / 57-g) chicken tenders
- Avocado oil cooking spray
- 2 slices turkey bacon
- 2 (9-ounce / 255-g) packages shaved Brussels sprouts
- 2 hardboiled eggs, chopped
- 1/2 cup unsweetened dried cranberries

For the Dressing:
- 3 tablespoons honey mustard
- 3 tablespoons extra-virgin olive oil
- 1/2 tablespoon freshly squeezed lemon juice

Nutrition:
- Calories: 467
- Fat: 20.1 g
- Protein: 35.1 g
- Carbohydrates: 36.9 g
- Fiber: 10.1 g
- Sugar: 14.0 g
- Sodium: 243 mg

Direction

To Make the Salad
- Preheat the oven to 425oF (220°C).
- Lightly coat the chicken tenders with cooking spray, then place them on a baking sheet and bake for 15 to 18 minutes.
- Meanwhile, heat a large skillet over medium-low heat. When hot, fry the bacon for 5 to 7 minutes until crispy. When the bacon is done, carefully remove it from the pan, and set it on a plate lined with a paper towel to drain and cool. Crumble when cool enough to handle.
- Cut the chicken tenders into even pieces. Divide the Brussels sprouts into four equal portions. Top each portion with one-quarter of the chopped eggs, crumbled bacon, dried cranberries, and 2 sliced chicken tenders.
- Drizzle an equal portion of dressing over each serving.

To Make the Dressing
- In a small bowl, whisk together the mustard, olive oil, and lemon juice.

SPINACH, PEAR, AND WALNUT SALAD

- Preparation time: 10 min
- Cooking time: 0 min
- Servings: 2

NUTRITION:

- Calories: 229
- Fat: 20.4 g
- Protein: 3.5 g
- Carbohydrates: 10.7 g
- Fiber: 3.4 g
- Sugar: 4.9 g
- Sodium: 644 mg

INGREDIENTS

- 2 tablespoons apple cider vinegar
- 1 teaspoon peeled and grated fresh ginger
- 1/2 teaspoon Dijon mustard
- 2 tablespoons extra-virgin olive oil
- 1/2 teaspoon sea salt
- 4 cups baby spinach
- 1/2 pear, cored, peeled, and chopped
- 1/4 cup chopped walnuts

DIRECTION

1. Combine the vinegar, ginger, mustard, olive oil, and salt in a small bowl. Stir to mix well.
2. Combine the remaining ingredients in a large serving bowl, then toss to combine well.
3. Pour the vinegar dressing in the bowl of salad and toss before serving.

Zucchini Salad with Ranch Dip

Preparation time: 5 min
Cooking time: 0 min
Servings: 4

INGREDIENTS

- 1 cup cottage cheese
- 2 tablespoons mayonnaise
- Juice of 1/2 lemon
- 2 tablespoons chopped fresh chives
- 2 tablespoons chopped fresh dill
- 2 scallions, white and green parts, finely chopped
- 1 garlic clove, minced
- 1/2 teaspoon sea salt
- 2 zucchinis, cut into sticks
- 8 cherry tomatoes

Nutrition:

- Calories: 92
- Fat: 4.1 g
- Protein: 7.1 g
- Carbohydrates: 6.9 g
- Fiber: 1.1 g
- Sugar: 5.3 g
- Sodium: 388 mg

DIRECTION

1. In a small bowl, mix the cottage cheese, mayonnaise, lemon juice, chives, dill, scallions, garlic, and salt.
2. Serve with the zucchini sticks and cherry tomatoes for dipping.

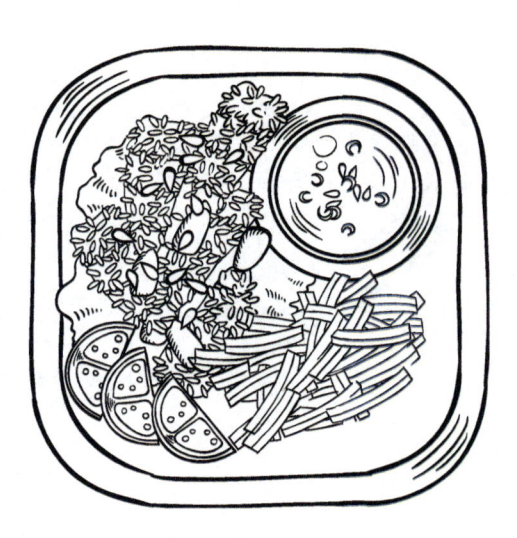

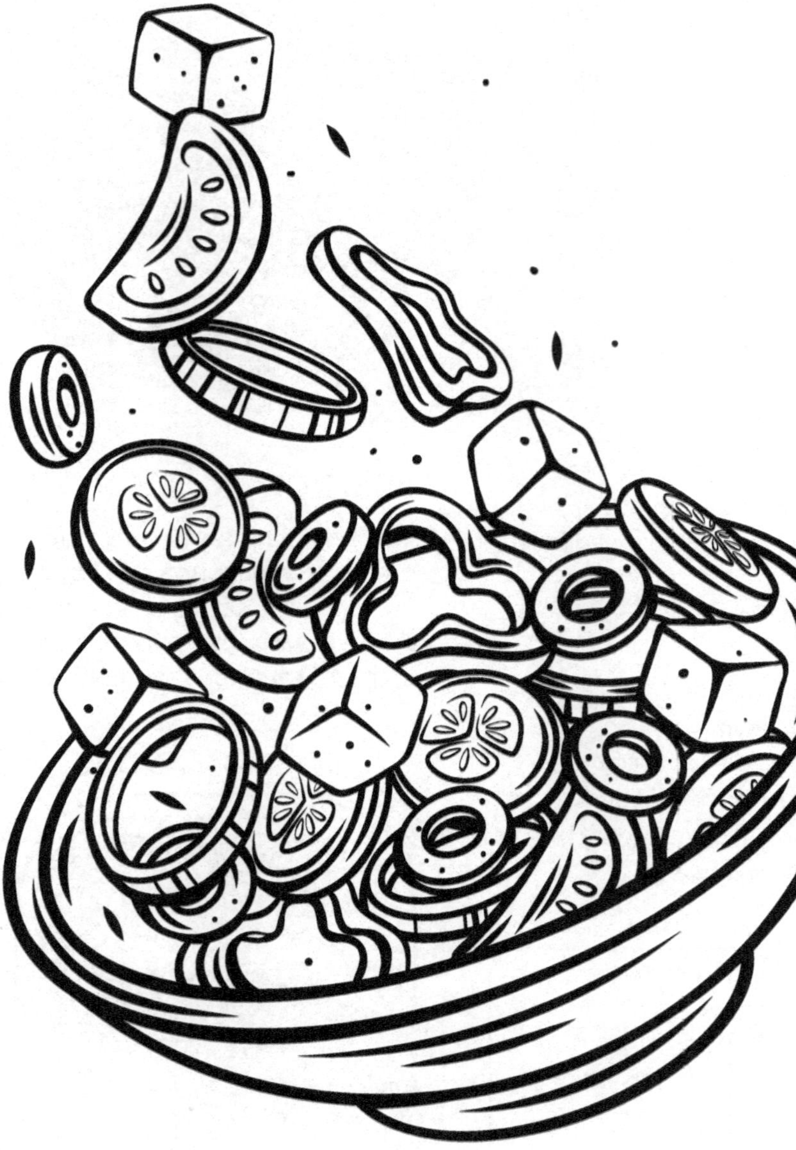

5
DESSERT RECIPES

Chocolate Ice Cream

Prep Time: 10 mins   **Cook Time:** 60 min   **Servings:** 2 portion

Ingredients:

- 1/2 cup Almond Milk, unsweetened
- 2 1/2 oz. Greek Yoghurt, fat-free
- 2 tbsp. Stevia
- 1/2 oz. Protein Powder
- 1 tsp. Vanilla Extract
- 1 tsp. Cocoa Powder, unsweetened

Direction

1. Place yogurt, almond milk, cocoa powder, stevia, and protein powder in a high-speed blender.
2. Blend them for few minutes or until you get a smooth mixture.
3. Place in the freezer to set.
4. Take out the ice cream every 30 seconds and blend. Repeat the procedure for about 2 hours until you get the right consistency without any ice blocks.
5. Serve and enjoy.

Nutrition:

- Calories: 151
- Carbohydrates: 1.5 g
- Proteins: 5 g
- Fat: 10 g
- Sodium: 328 mg

Chocolate Mousse

Prep Time : 10 mins   **Cook Time :** 5 mins   **Servings :** 4 portion

Ingredients :

- 1/4 cup Cocoa Powder, unsweetened
- 1 cup Heavy Whipping Cream
- 1 tsp. Vanilla Extract
- 1/4 cup Low-Carb Sweetener, powdered
- 1/4 tsp. Salt

Direction

1. Place the whipping cream in a large mixing bowl and whisk it with a mixer until you get stiff peaks.
2. Stir in the remaining ingredients and whisk until everything comes together.
3. Serve and enjoy.

Nutrition:

- Calories: 218
- Carbohydrates: 3 g
- Proteins: 2 g
- Fat: 23 g
- Sodium: 29 mg

Chia Pudding

Prep Time : 10 mins **Cook Time :** 0 min **Servings :** 1 portion

Ingredients :

- 2 tbsp. Chia Seeds
- 1 cup Almond Milk
- 1 tsp. Stevia, vanilla flavored

Direction

1. Mix the chia seeds and almond milk thoroughly until combined well.
2. Set it aside for overnight in the refrigerator.
3. Serve and enjoy. You can top with topping of your choice like berries, nuts, etc.

Nutrition:

- Calories: 151
- Carbohydrates: 1.5 g
- Proteins: 5 g
- Fat: 10 g
- Sodium: 328 mg

Keto Vanilla Mug Cake

Prep Time : 10 mins   **Cook Time :** 4hr20m   **Servings :** 4-6 portion

Ingredients :

- 1/4 tsp. Baking Powder
- 1 tbsp. Butter, melted
- 1 tsp. Vanilla Extract
- 2 tbsp. Cream Cheese
- 1 Egg
- 2 tbsp. Coconut Flour
- 6 Raspberries, frozen
- 1 tbsp. Low-Carb Sweetener, granulated

Direction

1. Place butter and cream cheese in a large mug and heat on high power for 20 seconds.
2. Spoon in coconut flour, baking powder, sweetener, and vanilla to it. Combine.
3. Add the egg to it and stir it again.
4. Scrape down the sides and press the six raspberries to it.
5. Heat the batter again for 1 minute and 20 seconds on high power.
6. Allow it to cool and set aside.

Nutrition:

- Calories: 342
- Carbohydrates: 4.5 g
- Proteins: 9 g
- Fat: 27 g
- Sodium: 17 mg

Tiramisu Shots

Prep Time : 5 mins   **Cook Time :** 10 min   **Servings :** 4 portion

Ingredients :

- 1 pack silken tofu
- 1 oz. dark chocolate, finely chopped
- 1/4 cup sugar substitute
- 1 teaspoon lemon juice
- 1/4 cup brewed espresso
- Pinch salt
- 24 slices angel food cake
- Cocoa powder (unsweetened)

Direction

1. Add tofu, chocolate, sugar substitute, lemon juice, espresso and salt in a food processor.
2. Pulse until smooth.
3. Add angel food cake pieces into shot glasses.
4. Drizzle with the cocoa powder.
5. Pour the tofu mixture on top.
6. Top with the remaining angel food cake pieces.
7. Chill for 30 minutes and serve.

Nutrition:

- Calories: 75;
- Carbohydrate: 12 g
- Protein: 2.9 g

Slow Cooker Peaches

Prep Time : 10 mins   **Cook Time :** 4hr20m   **Servings :** 4-6 portion

Ingredients :

- 4 cups peaches, sliced
- 2/3 cup rolled oats
- 1/3 cup Bisques
- 1/4 teaspoon cinnamon
- 1/2 cup brown sugar
- 1/2 cup granulated sugar

Direction

1. Spray the slow cooker pot with a cooking spray.
2. Mix oats, Bisques, cinnamon and all the sugars in the pot.
3. Add peaches and stir well to combine. Cook on low for 4-6 hours.

Nutrition:

- Calories: 617;
- Fat: 3.6 g
- Total carbs: 13 g
- Protein: 9 g

Keto Donuts

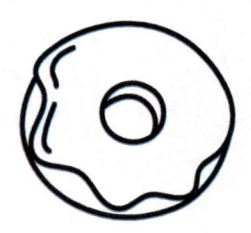

Prep Time : 5 mins   **Cook Time :** 0 mins   **Servings :** 4 portion

Ingredients :

- 1/2 Cup sifted almond flour
- 3 to 4 tablespoons coconut milk
- 2 Large eggs
- 2 to 3 tablespoons granulated stevia
- 1 Teaspoon Keto-friendly baking powder
- 1 Heap teaspoon apple cider vinegar
- 1 Pinch salt
- 1 and 1/2 Tablespoon sifted cacao powder
- 3 Teaspoons Ceylon cinnamon
- 1 Teaspoon powdered vanilla bean
- 1 Tablespoon grass-fed ghee
- 2 Tablespoons Coconut oil for greasing
- 4 Tablespoons of melted coconut butter with 1 to 2 teaspoons of coconut oil
- Edible rose petals, or shredded cacao

Nutrition:

- Calories: 122
- Fat: 6.8 g
- Carbohydrates: 13.5 g
- Fiber: 2.3 g
- Protein: 3 g

Direction

1. Preheat the oven to a temperature of about 350 degrees.
2. Grease a donut tray with the coconut oil.
3. Stir all together the sifted almond flour with the coconut milk, eggs, the granulated stevia, the Keto-friendly baking powder, the apple cider vinegar, the salt, the sifted cocoa powder, the Ceylon cinnamon, the powdered vanilla bean and the grass-fed ghee.
4. Mix your donut ingredients until they are evenly combined.
5. Divide the obtained batter into the donut moulds making sure to fill each to 3/4 full.
6. Bake for about 8 minutes; then remove the tray from the oven and carefully transfer it to a wire rack.
7. Serve and enjoy your donut or top it with the icing and the garnish of your choice.
8. Serve and enjoy your delicious treat!

Coconut Milk Pear Shake

Prep Time : 2 mins   **Cook Time :** 0 mins   **Servings :** 3-4 portion

Ingredients :

- 4 Ripe chopped pears
- 4 lettuce leaves finely torn into pieces
- 1/4 Cup unsweetened coconut milk
- 5 Dried and toasted Almonds
- 4 Leaves mint
- 2 Tablespoons unsweetened orange juice
- 1/2 Tablespoon apple sauce
- 5 ice cubes

Direction

1. Place the chopped pears in the blender.
2. Add the lettuce leaves.
3. Pour in the almond milk and the rest of the ingredients with the ice cubes.
4. Blend all of your ingredients for around 3 minutes.
5. Serve and enjoy!

Nutrition:

- Calories: 60
- Fat: 3 g
- Carbohydrates: 2.8 g
- Fiber: 1 g
- Protein: 3 g

Cocoa Mousse

Prep Time : 3 mins   **Cook Time :** 0 mins   **Servings :** 2 portion

Ingredients :

- 1 Cup Heavy Whipping coconut Cream
- 1/4 Cup sifted, unsweetened cocoa powder
- 1/4 Cup Swerve
- 1 Teaspoon Vanilla extract
- 1/4 Teaspoon kosher salt

Direction

1. Start by whisking the cream until it starts stiffening.
2. Add in the stevia, the vanilla and the salt, and whisk your ingredients very well.
3. Add the cocoa powder to your ingredients and whisk again.
4. Serve and enjoy your Cocoa mousse!

Nutrition:

- Calories: 218
- Fat: 23 g
- Carbohydrates: 5 g
- Fiber: 1 g
- Protein: 3 g

Coconut Ice Cream

Prep Time : 2 mins   **Cook Time :** 0 mins   **Servings :** 3-4 portion

Ingredients :

- 2 Cups canned coconut milk
- 1/3 Cup stevia
- 1/8 Teaspoon salt
- 1 1/2 tsp pure vanilla extract or vanilla bean paste

Direction

1. Make sure to use full-fat canned coconut milk.
2. You can also use the seeds of a vanilla bean instead of the extract.
3. Now, to make the ice cream, mix the milk with the Swerve the salt and the vanilla extract.
4. If you own an ice cream machine, you can simply churn by following the manufacturer's instructions.
5. Freeze the obtained mixture into ice cube trays, then blend in a blender on a high-speed; you can use a Vitamix, for example.
6. Freeze the ice cream for about 30 minutes.
7. Serve and enjoy your ice cream!

Nutrition:

- Calories: 283
- Fat: 21.5 g
- Carbohydrates: 5.1 g
- Fiber: 1.3 g
- Protein: 3.2 g

Fruit Pizza

Prep Time : 5 mins   **Cook Time :** 10 mins   **Servings :** 4 portion

Ingredients :

- 1 teaspoon maple syrup
- 1/4 teaspoon vanilla extract
- 1/2 cup coconut milk yogurt
- 2 round slices watermelon
- 1/2 cup blackberries, sliced
- 1/2 cup strawberries, sliced
- 2 tablespoons coconut flakes (unsweetened)

Direction

1. Mix maple syrup, vanilla and yogurt in a bowl.
2. Spread the mixture on top of the watermelon slice.
3. Top with the berries and coconut flakes.

Nutrition:

- Calories 70;
- Carbohydrate 14.6 g
- Protein 1.2 g

Choco Peppermint Cake

Prep Time : 5mins   **Cook Time :** 10 mins   **Servings :** 4 portion

Ingredients :

- Cooking spray
- 1/3 cup oil
- 15 oz. package chocolate cake mix
- 3 eggs, beaten
- 1 cup water
- 1/4 teaspoon peppermint extract

Direction

1. Spray slow cooker with oil.
2. Mix all the ingredients in a bcwl.
3. Use an electric mixer on medium speed setting to mix ingredients for 2 minutes.
4. Pour the mixture into the slow cooker.
5. Cover the pot and cook on low for 3 hours.
6. Let cool before slicing and serving.

Nutrition:

- Calories 185;
- Carbohydrate 27 g
- Protein 3.8 g

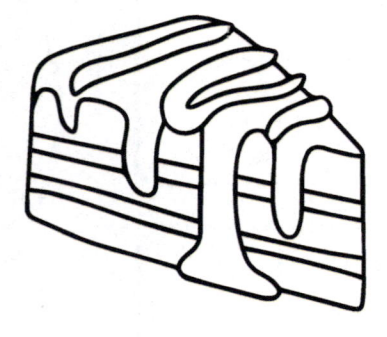

Roasted Mango

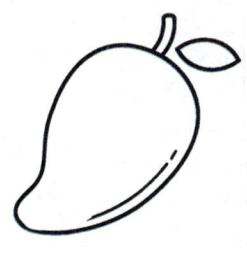

Prep Time : 5 mins   **Cook Time :** 10 mins   **Servings :** 4 portion

Ingredients :

- 2 mangoes, sliced
- 2 teaspoons crystallized ginger, chopped
- 2 teaspoons orange zest
- 2 tablespoons coconut flakes (unsweetened)

Direction

1. Preheat your oven to 350 degrees F.
2. Add mango slices in custard cups.
3. Top with the ginger, orange zest and coconut flakes.
4. Bake in the oven for 10 minutes.

Nutrition:

- Calories 89;
- Carbohydrate 20 g
- Protein 0.8 g

Roasted Plums

Prep Time : 5mins   **Cook Time :** 10 mins   **Servings :** 4 portion

Ingredients :

- Cooking spray
- 6 plums, sliced
- 1/2 cup pineapple juice (unsweetened)
- 1 tablespoon brown sugar
- 2 tablespoons brown sugar
- 1/4 teaspoon ground cardamom
- 1/2 teaspoon ground cinnamon
- 1/8 teaspoon ground cumin

Direction

1. Combine all the ingredients in a baking pan.
2. Roast in the oven at 450 degrees F for 20 minutes.

Nutrition:

- Calories 102;
- Carbohydrate 18.7 g
- Protein 2 g

Figs with Honey & Yogurt

Prep Time : 5 mins **Cook Time :** 10 mins **Servings :** 4 portion

Ingredients :

- 1/2 teaspoon vanilla
- 8 oz. nonfat yogurt
- 2 figs, sliced
- 1 tablespoon walnuts, chopped and toasted
- 2 teaspoons honey

Direction

1. Stir vanilla into yogurt.
2. Mix well.
3. Top with the figs and sprinkle with walnuts.
4. Drizzle with honey and serve.

Nutrition:

- Calories 157;
- Carbohydrate 24 g
- Protein 7 g

Printed in Great Britain
by Amazon